Love As The Stars Went Out.

- David Jones -

David Jones was born in 1989 in Liverpool, which is still his home. He studied English Language and Literature at the University of Liverpool, before specialising in Renaissance and Eighteenth Century Literature. He started writing at an early age, and has published four poetry books (Could You Ever Live Without?, Love And Space Dust, Love As The Stars Went Out and Highway Heart) and a novella called Death's Door. He is also a filmmaker, playwright and actor, and is currently completing work on a full length novel.

For more information on the writer, visit: www.storydj.com, twitter @djthedavid or on Facebook at https:// www.facebook.com/davidjoneswriter and @storydj Instagram. He also uploads weekly videos on youtube at http:// www.youtube.com/storydj.

"How strange to dream of you even when I am wide awake."

My thoughts were
Destroying me.
I tried not to think
But the silence
Was a killer too.

How strange
To dream of you
Even when
I am wide awake.

And then there
Are the songs
I cannot listen to
Without hearing
You.

I went to sleep
With music in my soul:
Drenched in the melody
Of every word
You spoke.

Everything is pure
At 4am.
Reality shivers
With the cold,
And my heart
Shivers with the
Memories of you.

Sometimes I sleep
Sometimes I wake.

Sometimes I speak
Sometimes I sigh.

Sometimes I think
Sometimes I don't.

Today I lived
But one day
I will die.

Life is too short
For all the lives
I have dreamed
Of living.

Whatever happens
To the dead words?

Sometimes I think
It is not the past
That haunts us,
But the words
We never dared
Speak.

Asleep or
Awake, I dream
Of you
All the same.

It did not
Kill me and
It did not
Make me stronger.

It simply was
And always will
Be scorched upon
My heart.

In the end
Even the stars
Choose destruction
Over life.

Your eyes
Stole all my words
Away.

I gave too much
Of myself until there
Was nothing left,
And then you were
Gone too because

Who can love a spectre
After all?

In some other life
We are standing
Side by side and
Laughing that,
In some other life

We are apart.

I keep finding
You in all
The old songs
I used to love.

I learned
A thousand lessons
In just
A moment
With you.

I did not speak
But I felt, I
Felt everything,
Every moment.
Your every breath
Fell like crashing
Thunder.

I am not coping.
It is these night time
Hours that tear
Me apart.

I held your hand
And felt the stars
Crackling beneath
Your skin.

Your name is
In the stars. I
Have breathed
You into the cosmos
So many times.

When I met you
The sky burned,
And so did I.

I breathed in
The night and felt
The stars
Fill up my soul.

I was missing you
Long before we
Even met.

You still live in
The silences
Between
My thoughts.

I wanted to vanish
So completely
That even I would
Not remember me:

No feelings, no
Memories, just
The freedom of
Oblivion.

And I am
Still haunted by
All the things
I could have
Been.

The moon
And the stars
Tried their best,
But I couldn't
Look away
From you.

Half the world
Is carrying
A broken heart.

Half the world
Is dreaming
Of being
Put together
Again.

We could
Be in love
For a billion
Life times
And I

Would still
Look at you
As if for
The first time.

I still look
At you as if
You put
The stars
Into the sky.

Every dream is real,
Even if it
Dies with
The daylight.

Give me all
Your dark thoughts
And give me all
Your pain.
We'll use them to
Make a blanket,
And together we'll
Survive the night.

No words, now.
I am tired, I want
To sleep and never
Dream, to be free
Of thoughts and
Fears and all.

In the graveyard
Of my heart stand
The tomb stones of all
The lives I could
Have lived and
All the people I might
Have been.

I want to
Fight for you
But I
Do not know
How and

The battle was
Lost long
Before
It began.

I am
Homesick
For
You.

This fire in my
Heart would blaze
Even at the bottom
Of the ocean.

Someone tell me
Why and how
I think these
Thoughts and
Feel these things.

I am a maze within
A maze, a desert
Sea of shifting
Sands, and even
The moon smiles
And sighs:

"I do not know.
I do not know."

I can't write
Or read or
Sing or think
Of even
Dream and it's
You
You
You.

A New Year's Haiku

The end of one year,
A new life hurrying in;
We can start again.

"Loving someone is one thing, but when loving them changes you, when they make you a better person, that's the real deal. When love makes you the best person you can ever be."

The butterflies in
My stomach were
Raising
Storms.

We met at
The end of the world,
And sat
Hand in hand as
The stars went out.

My heart
Broke with
The pain of
Being both
With and
Without
You.

6:32am.
Dawn.
No change.
Awake but
Dreaming
Of you.

I have said:

"I don't need you"

A hundred times, but
How can that be true
When I can't even stop
Talking about you?

In all of time,
I wonder how
Many lives I
Will have to
Live, until I

find my way
back to you

You may as well
Have tattooed
"What if?"
Across the skies,
For it was all
I ever thought.

All the
Killer words
In all the
Killer world

And I found:

"I love you."

I drank in
Your words and
Felt the poison
In my veins.

Tell me how
To begin, and I
Will tell you
How I love you
So.

I have never
Loved anything
Or anyone
Like this.

The deserts
Could turn
To seas, the
Cities to dust

And I would

Still be dreaming
Of you.

It was alcohol
Or you, but I
Was drunk
All the same.

She hit me like
The sun,
The moon,
The stars:
Full of light
But far away.

I packed my suitcase
And made my way,
Said a long goodbye
To yesterday,
But in my heart and
In my bones
The memories of you
Are etched in stone.

A memory is
A star,
Or a stain.

It was never enough,
Not any of it.
I dreamed
Of the world but
They handed me
A cage.

And nobody
Is winning the
War inside me.

The rivers
Bend and the
Stars come
Tumbling from
The sky

and
all because
i met you.

Tick tock
Goes the clock,
And whispers
That it was me
Who you
Forgot.

The moon
And the stars
Tried their best,
But I couldn't
Look away
From you.

I don't want
A fairytale,
I just want
You.

And I have
Always felt that
People made
A far greater
Impression on me
Than I could ever
Make on them.

The problem is
I do not want to forget.
Despite all the pain,
The hurt, I still want
To remember you.

I still want my heart
To beat to the sound
Of your name.

Our shadows
Are still dancing
Like spectres in
My dreams.

To be alone
With you as
The world spins
And the stars
Chase each other
Across the skies.

And in the end
There will be the day,
There will be the night,
And there will be us.

Love does not
Care.
Cupid is a
Thoughtless,
Reckless archer.

A Christmas Eve Haiku.

Christmas Eve at last,
That night of myth and magic;
Time lasts forever.

Death looked
So alone.
How could I
Not reach out
To him?

I wandered alone
Through the deserted
Streets of my heart,
Hoping to find
You there.

And I knew
At once
How much
It would hurt
To finally
Let you go.

There was
Heaven before
My eyes, but
Hell behind them.

Even the
Stars in
Dead space
Whisper:

"What if?"

I chased you from
My thoughts
But never
My dreams.

The stars speak
In a hidden language:
They write for us
All, but each of us
Reads a different
Story.

I tried
To hide inside
Myself, but
That was where
All the danger
Was.

And I began
To miss a life
That never
Even existed.

The End

I looked at you and felt the stars go out in my heart.

I tried so hard
To care, but
All I heard was
The echoing
Emptiness
In my soul.

Trapped
Somewhere
Between wanting
To forget
And wanting
To hold on.

Too tired
To sleep,
Too tired
To cry,
Too tired
To be.

I looked up into
The dark of the sky
And knew what
It is to want
Nothing, nobody;
To have no words,
No thoughts, no
Dreams, just an
Endless canvas of
Night upon night
Upon

Night.

The memories
Won't die,
But I will.

One day
The dark behind
My eyes
Will become
My only sky.

How many times
Can I say
"It will be better tomorrow?

Too little living and
Too much thinking:
My thoughts are
Eating me from
The inside out.

Perhaps I was
Never real.
At 4am, when
The sky is
Pale and the
Light is feeble,
I can feel
Myself fading
Into the oblivion
Of the dawn.

I misplaced my heart
In some forgotten
Corner. It was only
You who helped me
Find it again.

They saved
My body with
Medicine and
Pills but forgot
My soul, so that
I lived, but
Died.

We were
Almost
Fine,
Almost
Happy.

How terrifying
It is
To be
Happy.

Of all the lives
In all the worlds,
I would always
Find this one,
Here with
You.

My feelings
Bled me
Dry.

Thoughts
Punching holes
In the fabric
Of my
Mind.

And all those
Places in my
Dreams still
Seem so real.

I am wishing
My life away,
Wishing
For you.

If only the rain
Could wash away
The memories
And sweep
Yesterday into
The sea.

The God and the Bridge.

Once upon a time there was a God and a mountain. From his sky high throne The God would gaze down upon creation through contented eyes, watching as men and women no larger than ants scuttled this way and that as they eased themselves into the reality of their existence. In these first, halcyon days of civilisation the God would occasionally intervene. Sometimes he would see fit to speak to his people directly, at other times he would deliver a prophet into their midst or, if the fancy took him, he would perform impressive miracles. The God would part the clouds with a breath, and smile as the people constructed temples in his honour, burned incense and whispered prayers into the deep blue of the sky. Imperious above the city, the mountain itself became a shrine, and worshippers congregated beneath its unassailable slopes to lay flowers, emblems, and chant the name of their deity. In the dead of the night lanterns would be lit and given to the air so that they drifted up to the summit in his honour. The God was satisfied. He saw no reason to continue his interventions and miracles, for the people seemed both able to care for themselves, and devoted enough to continue his worship without any coaxing. Instead he took more permanently to the seclusion of his mountain top retreat, where he remained in uncommunicative silence, peering down the slope into that very first settlement which would, in time, grow into a great capital of criss-crossing roads and sky scrapers striving for the heavens.

The civilisation did indeed grow and swell for it was glutted upon time, learning and progress. Outlaying villages took root, flourished into towns and then cities in their own right. The population spread ever further from its cradle, and entire settlements beyond the gaze of the God sprung spontaneously into life. All the while, he watched the city with fascination as it grew masterful in engineering, in medicine, in writing, in sciences and the arts. Centuries as fleeting as moments sped by, and the metropolis bore little resemblance to that first sculpted at the hands of its creator. His worship continued, albeit without the dedicated zeal of those early, long dead men and women, but the God was unconcerned, and reclined quite happily upon his throne. So much time had elapsed since his last intervention that it seemed improper to make a sudden and dramatic return to the world of the mortals. Besides, the people still recalled him. There were great cathedrals amongst the sky scrapers, the same prayers of old were spoken, and the same hymns. For many centuries events proceeded in this easy manner. The God was untroubled and carefree, until one day he caught sight of something monstrous: the people were building a bridge.

This development had gone unnoticed for some time. The God had been lost in contemplation, and when he finally lowered his gaze to the city, many of the foundations of the bridge were already firmly in place. Great pillars as tall as skyscrapers were nestled amongst the cities rooftops and long, metal sheets had been placed on top to form the beginnings of a gigantic bridge. The God rose to his feet and hurried to the edge of the summit. He squinted through the clouds in disbelief, but there was no denying the truth. The bridge was constructed at such an angle that upon completion it would stretch from the city streets up to the mountain top. As though they sought to hide this appalling vision from him, the clouds quickly crowded between the God and the ground, but he blew them aside and continued to stare, wide eyed and aghast, as machines and workers toiled away on the bridge even as he watched. Appalled at this new and unexpected blasphemy, the God staggered back from the edge and seated himself on his throne, but even from there the foundations of the bridge were plainly visible. The God was shaken. At first he put his head in his hands and wondered whether he would weep, but in time sorrow at this strange insult quickly transformed into rage, and he paced furiously about the mountain top, kicking the rocks and beating his fists against the air until a mighty tempest was stirred.

"Ah!" he cried as he saw the winds rising "This is a pleasing omen. I will smite them and reduce their bridge to ruin!"

The God had worked himself into a fine frenzy of aggression, and the idea of smiting struck him as especially enticing. The more he considered it, though, the less appealing it became. Incalculable spans of time had elapsed since he had last intervened in the lives of the mortals. He had not smote anything or anyone for longer than he could recall. Perhaps this was no time for panic after all. To deliver a mighty thunderbolt or raise an inferno would only heap fuel upon their curiosity for the mountain top, and he would find himself knocking down a new bridge every day.

"And besides" he thought "I am safe up here. It will take them many lifetimes to build a bridge as tall as this mountain. By then something will have happened to change their minds."

In the first of his predictions the God was proved correct, for the building of the bridge could not be completed in a single generation. His second prognosis was sorely inaccurate though, for nothing occurred to bring about a monumental change in the heart's of the people, and they continued to build. After the initial flurry of activity the construction of the bridge slowed, but never ceased. Successive generations added further pillars, and the structure ascended ever higher, drawing closer and closer to the mountain top. Stricken alternately with sorrow and fury, the God could only pace about his palace, both raging at and lamenting the audacity of the people beneath him. In his more lucid moments he noted how the number of places of worship in the city were dwindling, and he was well aware that they were doing so in direct correlation to the progress and size of the bridge. Many centuries had vanished into dust since one of the lanterns had fluttered up to the mountain top, and nor had there been tributes or shrines at its base for longer than he dared recall. Despite all this, the God still harboured the rapidly diminishing hope that something dramatic would change the people's minds, that they would run out of money or enthusiasm and the abhorrent project would cease before it reached him.

On one particularly frightful day the bridge finally pierced the clouds, so that the God was no longer even granted the peace of mind usually associated with an overcast sky. It was on this day that he finally surrendered all hope of the abandonment of the bridge, for the project had already spanned many generations. The bridge was so near to the mountain top now that he could see the workers as they toiled. No longer the size of ants, it would not be long until he would be able to hear their voices and discern their features. For the briefest of moments the God was genuinely afraid, and from that day forward he fell into a deep melancholy. The bridge continued its inexorable and inevitable advance until it was level with the mountain top. Supported by gigantic concrete pillars of ascending height, it towered up first through the clouds and then into the dizzying depths of the pale blue heavens. It would only require a few more days of labour to finally cross the divide and deliver the people into the abode of the God, who could scarce believe his eyes, for the people had erected a structure equal in stature to his mountain. There was no way to avert the oncoming tragedy, and as the final stages of construction fell seamlessly, easily into place, the God slumped miserably and helplessly into a corner and commenced his wait for the inevitable with a heavy heart.

"If they are coming to destroy or depose me" he said aloud, his voice faltering "Then they shall find themselves in all kinds of peril."

Even the God had lost faith in his words though, and before long the final sections of the bridge were in place, forging a direct link between the earth and the mountain top. The dreadful moment had finally arrived and the God recoiled, half in horror, half in anger, as the first human steps were set upon his plateau. The eyes of the mortal darted this way and that, fell squarely upon the God but seemed to gaze directly through him. There was no wide eyed awe, no gasp of exhilaration - there was certainly no divine admiration, only a blank, faintly disappointed stare and a frown.

"Why, there is nothing here" said the human.

Almost at once, there was a woman at his side. She too looked directly at the God and then around, her eyes passing over the pillars, the throne and all the sumptuous glories of the Heavenly palace.

"It is as I have always suspected: nothing" she said miserably "Come and admire our folly, for it is just a mountain top like any other."

At this beckoning call, a mass of people came pouring across the bridge and a crowd began to gather. Men, women and children, some of whom the God recognised as having been directly involved in the construction of the bridge, rushed across it and thronged about the mountain top.

"It's empty. What a fine waste of time this has proved to be. I said as much before we got here."

"Nothing. An empty mountain top and nothing more. I could have told you that long ago."

"I had always thought it. There is absolutely nothing here."

Thus continued the dissatisfied choir of voices until there was not an inch of the mountain top which was not occupied by a city dweller. Those voices, initially disgruntled at the thwarting of their curiosity, grew increasingly aggressive, and in no time at all the people were clamouring for the bridge to be torn down. The city mayor was especially displeased. He had been no advocate of the generation spanning bridge project. If the scheme had not endured for so long he would surely have cancelled it upon taking office, but nobody wanted to be remembered as the one responsible for undoing the work of countless ages. Finally vindicated in his feelings, the mayor nonetheless derived little pleasure from his victory:

"We have already squandered ample time and money on this, damnable fools that we are. Knocking it down again would only cost us more. I say we leave it here as a testament to our shameful credulity."

This suggestion was greeted with a chorus of low, approving murmurs.

"I expect I could build a tourist attraction up here" one voice chimed.

"Some type of coffee shop" said another "With a viewing platform."

The mayor was highly satisfied with this, for at least they could recoup some of their fiscal losses.

"We will have a planning meeting" he announced "And set upon some scheme for the future."

Now that the emptiness of the mountain top had been confirmed, and the long toiled over bridge had simultaneously been completed and rendered useless, the people did not linger. The crowd fragmented, dispersed and made its way back to earth. The mayor and some town planners delayed a little longer, grumbling amongst themselves at the squandered money, but nonetheless a little optimistic for profit in the future. They were the last to leave. They took measurements here and there, wondered about plans and materials, before returning to the bridge. And with that they left the deserted mountain top.

THE END.

MORE BOOKS FROM DAVID JONES

Love & Space Dust. A Poetry Anthology.

Love & Space Dust is a poetry anthology exploring love and eternity. Timeless poetry of feeling and emotion, Love & Space Dust carries readers on a journey through love, life and relationships, and then far beyond, into the stars and the far flung galaxies, where all that remains of the feelings we once felt and the lives we once lived is love and space dust.

"After spending over ten years in a literature club and hearing/reading more poems than I could count, I thought I had seen it all. I have never been so wrong. Love and Space Dust contains so many beautifully written poems that brought tears to my eyes that I didn't put my Kindle down until I had read every single one of them at least twice." Amazon.de Customer Review.

"Lovely book." Amazon.com Customer Review

"I really enjoy all of the poems. They make you feel like never before. By far some of my favorite poems." Amazon.com Customer Review.

"LOVED LOVED LOVED THIS!!" Goodreads Review.

"These poems are so full of Pain and Darkness, but so full of Hope and Light." Amazon.de Customer Review.

"This book is absolutely amazing and i hope there will be more to come!" Amazon.com Customer Review

"Love this book so much!" Goodreads Review.

"Made me smile and moved me to tears." Amazon.co.uk Customer Review.

Could You Ever Live Without? A Poetry Anthology.

Poems of feeling and experience, the anthology encompasses all of life and beyond: death, the universe, hopes, dreams, love, loss - all of existence contained in one work. Poetry that captures both moments and lifetimes, memories and hopes, reality and dreams. Poems to identify with, poems of life.

"Take it from a non-poetry reader: this book is a gem, destined to become timeless." Amazon Customer Review.

"Loved the poems, a very great read. Once I started reading it was hard to stop." Amazon Customer Review.

"This book is beautiful. It's one of my most cherished possessions." Amazon Customer Review.

"Not all poetry is worth reading. This is." Amazon Customer Review.

"A great reflection of the deeper thoughts from this generation." Amazon Customer Review.

"Beautiful collection of poetry, I'm not an avid poetry reader but this book is absolutely stunning."
Amazon.co.uk Customer Review.

"Everytime I read this book I find new meanings."
Goodreads Review.

Death's Door. A novella of love, life and death.

"She was like the dawn, insubstantial and somehow transient, as though she would fade from reality at any moment."

Every day the villagers watch as Death, a spectral suit of black armour mounted upon a horse, rides through the valley beneath their mountain top home. After a lifetime living on the edge of Death's domain, his close proximity is neither terrible or threatening, rather he has become a simple fact of life and a familiar neighbour. Nothing seems to change until one night a young boy, alone in the meadows beneath a summer moon, watches a mysterious figure in white approaching the village through the tall grass.

"A spectacular novella, a quick read but engaging and thoughtful. The story carries you as swift as death's horse does." Amazon.com Customer Review.

"Buy this book! Great teen-based book. Even better for post teen (aka 55 year old father) reader." Amazon.com Customer Review.

"This book quickly became my forever favorite. You will not regret buying it. Although it's about death himself, it has so much to teach about life." Amazon.com Customer Review.

Highway Heart. My newest poetry collection.

Highway Heart is a collection of over one hundred poems on relationships, life and the universe. The theme is journeys - the travel we undertake in life, the type of internal travel which traces roads inside our hearts.

Half an exploration of the difficulties of finding the right path in life, and half a bitter sweet celebration of the myriad of strange, exciting, heartbreaking and unexpected roads we discover for ourselves, Highway Heart is above all else the poetic tale of a journey.

"This is one of the greatest works I've ever read. This is truly, truly, a masterpiece. I hope it gets more recognition in the future. Please, please read it, it will touch the deepest parts of your heart." Amazon.com Review.

And Coming Soon...

A full length novel by David Jones exploring themes of love, eternity, the nature of the universe and history.

"When all of this is over, will our atoms play amongst the stars? Will we dance and laugh through the galaxies? Will we be happy at last?"

For further information and news on the novel please visit:

Twitter: @djthedavid
Instagram: @storydj
Youtube: youtube.com/storydj
Facebook: facebook.com/davidjoneswriter

Made in the USA
Las Vegas, NV
19 September 2024

95508266R00069